Drawing on the Power of Resonance in Writing

By David Farland

ISBN: 148491273X

ISBN-13: 978-1484912737

Table of Contents

Introduction 5
What is Resonance? 7
Three Types of Resonance 18

    Resonance within a Genre 18
    Resonance with Life....................18
    Resonance with Emotional Needs..............20

      Communicating Resonance to an
      Audience.......................................21

      Cover Art......................................21
      Story Title.....................................22
      Settings 24
      Motifs 25
      Characters 25
      Shared Experience.........................26

Weaving it all Together 28
    A Case Study in Using Resonance:
    Tolkien...29

      Echoing Other Works: Der Ring des
      Nibelung and The Lord of the Rings.31
    Resonance with Names 36
    Resonating with Other Works...................45
    Resonating with Universal Experiences.....55
    Internal Resonance.......................59

      Language in The Lord of the Rings 65

      In Conclusion................................79

Resonance within a Genre 80
Resonance Outside of Tolkien 87
Resonance and You 89
In Conclusion 94
Ways to Draw Upon Resonance 96

Introduction

A few years ago, I was asked to speak at a writing conference. The conference had been running for twenty years, and the administrator said, "We've covered just about every topic that I can think of over the past twenty years. Is there anything that you can think of that we haven't discussed?"

Immediately I suggested, "Well, of course one of the most important skills for a writer to master is the proper use of resonance."

The administrator was taken aback and asked, "What is resonance?"

Then it struck me. I had *never* heard any writer discuss resonance in writing at any conference. I'd never read a book or article on the topic. I'd never had one of my writing instructors discuss it. As far as I could tell, they were completely in the dark.

Instead of learning about resonance in one grand discourse, I picked up on the topic in bits and pieces. I'd read a brief mention about it in an article written by a master editor. An agent once spoke about it directly. I overheard a *New York Times* bestselling author try to explain the concept to a new writer, and T.S. Eliot touched upon it as he struggled to write works that were woven into the tapestry of literature as a whole. Mostly I had learned about it in Hollywood while working with directors.

But I've never heard novelists or writing instructors even mention the topic.

When I went to that writing conference years ago, perhaps forty writers attended my class. Many of them had studied the craft for decades. So I asked, "How many of you know what resonance is?" I was met by blank stares. Only one author had even heard the term, and she couldn't tell me what it meant.

All successful writers use resonance to enhance their stories by drawing power from stories that came before, by resonating with their readers' experiences, and by resonating within their own works.

In this book, you'll learn exactly what resonance is and how to use it to make your stories more powerful. You'll see how it is used in literature and other art forms, and how one writer, J. R. R. Tolkien, mastered it in his work.

What is Resonance?

In the field of music, a musical refrain is said to "resonate" when it "draws power by repeating that which has come before." Beethoven's Fifth Symphony is a masterpiece of resonance, and it is so well known that you may be able to listen to it in your head from memory:

Da, da, da, dum.
Da, da, da, dum. . . .

In case you can't play it in your head, search for it online.

As you listen to the symphony, you'll hear how Beethoven starts with a simple theme, repeating the same four notes twice, and then he has a change-up and expands upon that theme. He does this dozens of times, coming up with variation after variation, eventually seeming to abandon the theme altogether.

Indeed, a few minutes into the symphony there is a shocking moment where we realize that we have come full circle. Beethoven returns to the original theme, playing louder and more boldly than before. In music, when a refrain gains power by repeating something that has gone before, we say that it *resonates*.

But the same thing happens in literature. We feel powerful emotions when we read a book that somehow resembles other works that we love. For example, you may read a new author and discover that the author's world is similar to one that you've visited in literature and loved before. If you're a fan of the pirating world in *Treasure Island,* you might find that you really like Tim Powers's *On Stranger Tides.* You'll almost instantly feel a great affinity for Tim's work.

In a similar way, a tale may also resonate when it evokes powerful emotions by drawing upon the reader's own past experience. For example, a woman who has been divorced may read a passage in a novel and realize, "Wow, this author has really been through it, too. We really do have a lot in common."

There are literally hundreds of ways to create resonance—through voice, tone, characterization, imagery, setting, or simply by referring to popular works, by bringing common experiences to life, and so on.

To the reader, a story that resonates powerfully may seem especially significant or rich—much more so than a tale that doesn't resonate.

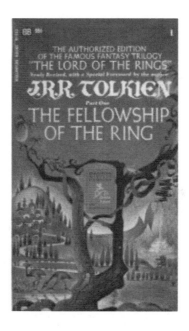

Readers often become fans of a genre after discovering one defining work in that genre. When I was a teen, I read Tolkien's *The Lord of the Rings*. I enjoyed the book so much that I began looking for similar titles. At the time, there was no such thing as a "fantasy genre," but I hungered for books like *Lord of the Rings*. I wanted to recreate the experience of reading it. So I tried Ursula K. LeGuin's *The Wizard of Earthsea*, Patricia McKillip's *The Riddlemaster of Hed*, and Fritz Leiber's *Fafhrd and the Gray Mouser*, among hundreds of other works.

Eventually, when I ran out of fantasy novels to read, I began to write my own. *A Wizard in Halflight*, one of my first tales, which I started writing at the age of 17, told the exploits of a young boy going to a high school to study wizardry.

Each time that I read a good fantasy, I found some new little nugget in the fantasy genre that seemed delicious to me. By doing so, I gained a deeper and broader appreciation for the genre as a whole.

You're much the same. Whatever your favorite genre is, you can probably trace your love for it back to one single book that really moved you.

Many people became vampire fans as children by watching old horror movies. Later they expanded upon this by reading Anne Rice. You may have loved Buffy the Vampire Slayer. When Stephenie Meyer came out with *Twilight*, she played upon the works that preceded her, but she also expanded upon the genre in such a way that she brought in an entire new generation of readers. With that, vampire fiction took off to unprecedented heights in popularity, and suddenly we had a piece of *Twilight* fan fiction, *50 Shades of Grey*, become a hit.

Do you see how the genre grows in leaps from a base of fans? Each succeeding work is like a mushroom, rising up from the remains of what grew before.

So readers of romance might begin in high school by reading Emily Brontë's *Wuthering Heights,* go on to *Jane Eyre,* and begin developing a taste for romance. Very often, readers of romance will fall in love with books set in a particular historical period—the Regency Romances—where the genre began, but then will move on to more modern eras.

Historically, we've seen a number of genres develop due to one great work. Thus, you can look at something like the success of the film *Pirates of the Caribbean* and trace the genre back in time first to the rides at Disneyland in the 1960s, and from there on back to pirate books and movies of the past— from the films of Errol Flynn in the 1920s, to Robert Louis Stevenson's hit *Treasure Island* in 1883, from there to *Swiss Family Robinson* in 1812, and from there to *Robinson Crusoe,* first published in 1718. Each of these bestsellers resonated with huge hits from the past, and thus built up a larger fan base.

So readers are often searching for something that moves them in a familiar way.

As they grow more sophisticated in their tastes, widening their interests, the reader begins to look for something a little different. In other words, they want something similar— but better.

Thus, a reader of Westerns may say, "I'm tired of Zane Grey. I wonder what new authors are out there?" And he may discover Larry McMurtry's *Lonesome Dove*.

Readers crave something different, but not completely different.

As writers, we find that entire "genres" or "sub-genres" grow up around great novels. As new genres develop, over the centuries, hundreds of different types of code words, phrases, settings, and standard character types begin to creep into the field.

For example, if you're writing a romance, do you say that your hero has "gray" eyes or "grey" eyes? The answer, of course, is that he has "grey" eyes. Why? Because Emily Brontë's Heathcliffe had "grey" eyes, and thus the British spelling became preferred. It has stronger resonance with romance readers.

As a new writer, it's important to become familiar with these codes, these motifs. Readers will think that you're ignorant if you don't know the standards. For example, I recently read a novel by a mainstream writer who tried to dabble in science fiction. In it, she had an instantaneous communication device. She called it something like an "ICD." However, by doing so, she embarrassed herself in front of real science fiction aficionados. In the genre, such a device is known as an *ansible*. The word was coined by Ursula K. LeGuin in 1966 for her novel *Rocannon's World*. By not knowing this, the author revealed that she was a pretender. In effect, she was "slumming." So the novel died without real critical or financial success, despite the author's skill as a stylist.

In the same way, we have "code words" that creep into every genre of fiction. When I used to judge for the Writers of the Future Contest, every few months I would get a story that started like this:

> Joe, John, and Dave are sitting in a bar, drinking cool beers, brought to them by a big-chested waitress. They're jawing about things. "How's work?" Joe says. "Oh, you know, same ol' stuff," John says. "Say, have you seen Tina lately," Dave asks John.

(This banter goes on for a page or two.)

> Suddenly, the door to the bar bursts open, and a dwarf walks in. "Dwarf!" all three men suddenly shout, as they leap up from their stools and draw their swords.

As a reader, you might wonder, "Say what? They're drawing swords?"

Do you see what is wrong here? Nothing in the text indicated that this was a fantasy world. The author began with a description befitting any modern-day bar in Texas. But in fantasy we have a secret language, inspired by Tolkien and others, that lets us know that we're in a different time, a different world, where men wear swords and attack dwarves on sight. Using this language signals that the author is writing for a fantasy reader.

How would you then as an author address this problem?

First of all, the characters' names can't be Joe, John, and Dave. They have to sound like fantasy characters. So let's try Theron, Wulf, and Sir Giles.

Second, they're sitting in an *inn*, not in a bar.

They aren't drinking "cold beer," they're guzzling "frothy mugs of ale."

Instead of a "big-chested waitress," the brew is offered up by a "buxom serving wench."

When the men talk about their day, they don't say, "How's the boss treatin' ya?" Instead, one might ask, "Is Lord Hebring faring well?" And so on.

All of this prepares us for the moment when the dwarf walks in, and the three city guards suddenly draw swords ringing from their scabbards.

The truth is that if you as an author are not aware of the conventions and vocabulary of the genre that you're trying to write in, you will fail. Your readers will feel uneasy about your work, the critics who are familiar with the genre will lambaste you, and you will bomb at the bookstore.

Sometimes, authors get the wild notion that "Writing romance would be so easy," or "If I just moonlighted by writing a fantasy novel, I could write so much better than the rest of those idiots." It doesn't work that way.

You have to write in a field that you know. You have to love what you're doing. If you don't, the chances are almost zero that you will succeed.

The literary agent Richard Curtis once pointed this out. He said that over the years he has known dozens of authors who have gone slumming, but they almost never succeed in launching a new career. *Why? Because usually the author isn't familiar with the genre. He or she doesn't understand what resonates with readers. They don't know the secret conventions, don't understand what makes that work delicious to the reader.*

Almost every author falls into the trap of writing outside his area of expertise, it seems. I learned to love fantasy and science fiction when I was young. I have written successfully in both fields, becoming an international bestseller. But a few years ago, I got the urge to write a historical novel. "How hard can it be?" I asked myself. It wasn't as if I were creating new worlds, new societies. All that I had to do was writing about real people, living in a real world.

I soon found that writing a historical is grinding work. Yes, it was based upon a lot of first-hand accounts, but there were so many arguments about what really happened, I had to do two years of research in my spare time just to come up with my own version of the event. There were plenty of holes even in the best-researched account. Then I had to try to recreate the voices of my protagonists by drawing upon the flimsiest evidence—and I had to make them sound historically accurate. In order to flesh out their world, I had to draw upon newspapers, books, first-hand accounts, and military documents. Writing the novel required travel to museums, and stops along 1300 miles of prairies as I followed my characters' trail. In order to recreate their experience, I even braved a blizzard atop the Rocky Mountains. The novel, *In the Company of Angels*, went on to win an award for the "Best Book of the Year," but writing it was maybe the hardest thing I've ever done.

Here's what I learned: writing *well* in any genre is excruciating! If you're going to write, write in a genre that you love, so that writing will become a labor of love—not a chore.

I've pointed out what resonance is, but there is another point that I need to make about it. When you "create" any tale, you will subconsciously draw the story from *somewhere*. Researchers into the imagination don't believe that we can actually create worlds, societies, characters, and incidents out of thin air. Instead, the human mind pulls odd little tidbits from our past experience, and we fabricate our tales based upon that. In other words, whether you're trying to create resonance or not, you're still doing it. Some authors get lucky. They naturally create a work that resonates strongly without realizing what they've done.

My goal here is to train you to consider what you're doing, and learn to see resonance as the powerful tool that it is.

Three Types of Resonance

Resonance within a Genre

When you read a book that affects you powerfully, you'll be likely to buy a story that reminds you of it. This is true regardless of whether the story be Steinbeck's *Of Mice and Men*, Austen's *Pride and Prejudice*, Shakespeare's *Macbeth*, or Dickens's *A Christmas Carol*.

Most books that you buy resonate with some other work that you've enjoyed. You almost never make a conscious connection, but it is there. You tend to choose books that suit your developing tastes.

Resonance with Life

However, you should also be aware that we buy books that resonate with our own lives. For example, readers subconsciously gravitate to characters who are about their own age and sex. Thus, young women tend to like stories about young women, while young men like stories about teenage boys.

You can also resonate within a setting. If you set a story about a detective in a major city—let's say New York—you will find that people from that city are much more likely to buy your book. They feel a personal connection to the work that outsiders don't.

Entire cultures resonate. Recently I went to a large international book fair in Frankfurt, Germany, where thousands of publishers from around the world congregated. In many countries, I found that books from Western cultures simply "didn't translate." Want to know how well *Twilight* has done in Oman, or the Ukraine, or Indonesia? The chances are that it hasn't been translated at all. The entire lifestyle is so alien to people in those countries, that most of our literature just doesn't translate easily.

But there are other ways to resonate with life besides just the age of the protagonist or by choosing the setting. Years ago, I was asked by the chief editor at Scholastic to help choose the "next big book" for the year, the one that they would put all of their advertising muscle behind. I chose an unknown book called *Harry Potter*. The editor said that her marketing department didn't share my enthusiasm for the book: it was too long for a middle-grade audience. But I pointed out that it had several things going for it. One powerful draw was that every child in most of the world has to go to school. Adults feel that universal conflicts revolve around death, taxes, and love. But for children, the universals are bullies, inscrutable teachers, and being chained to a desk.

In short, almost every child in the world would find that Harry's experiences at Hogwarts resonated with their own life.

Resonance with Emotional Needs

We often choose the genre of fiction that we do because we are seeking to create a positive emotional experience.

The primary emotional draw of a book is so powerful that bookstores and libraries tend to arrange their shelves according to the emotion that the book arouses. Stores typically have shelves for "Romance," "Drama," "Mystery," "Horror," "Adventure," "Humor" and so on.

We could do a better job of arranging the books if we carried the practice further. One wise editor in the 1950s struggled to get fantasy and science fiction categorized as "wonder" literature in bookstores and libraries, since both genres promise to fulfill the same emotional need of wonder for readers.

Communicating Resonance to an Audience

When I worked in Hollywood, directors would often seek to have their works resonate with the monumental works in their field. They might say, "For this scene, I want a cool castle—sort of like Disney's palace, but not quite the same." They wanted the viewer to feel a connection, but not recognize that too consciously.

There are dozens of ways to create resonance. Let's go over just a few.

Cover Art

One of the first things that draws a reader into a story is the cover. If you pick up a romance novel, you want a picture that suggests romance—perhaps a man and woman hugging. If you want horror, something dark and sinister might be more apropos.

My own fantasy novels have covers by Darrell Sweet and look like other fantasy novels—with medieval characters on the cover, along with a few monsters. Sweet of course is famous for painting book covers for

Terry Brooks and Robert Jordan, two of our best-sellers of all time.

So when readers look at my novels, they are immediately reminded of books by those authors. Now, do I write like either of them? Not much. I write epic fantasy in a medieval setting, but I don't have a lot of the Tokienesque trappings that Brooks and Jordan have. Still, readers who like the work of these bestselling authors are likely to pick up my books based upon the style of the cover art.

Once, I heard Darrell Sweet mention that one of his books, *Ogre, Ogre,* had outsold all others. So when writing my novel *Wizardborn,* I put in a scene that would resonate with a part of *Ogre, Ogre.* Sweet picked up on it and created the exact scene that I wanted—and the book quickly became a bestseller.

Story Title

Resonance in titles is so important, that at one time it was considered "a must" for a mainstream writer to try to find something that would resonate with a reader's wider experience. Titles taken from the bible were popular. Thus, Hemingway once read through the bible more than once looking for a title that bible readers would be familiar with. It wasn't until one of his friends, John Steinbeck, recommended the passage "the sun also rises upon the just and the unjust" that Hemingway found his title.

Some authors go to absurd lengths to find titles that resonate for readers. When I was young I loved the book *The Swiss Family Robinson*. But even at the age of twelve I had to wonder, "Why was a Swiss family named *Robinson*?"

Even as a child I knew that the appendage "son" is commonly used by Danes, not the Swiss. It wasn't until a few years later that I realized that the writer was trying to use resonance to draw upon another book about a famous castaway, Daniel Defoe's *Robinson Crusoe*, which is often regarded as the first novel in the English language. Reading it would have been a must for every English schoolboy in the 1800s. The name "Robinson" had resonance. In fact, when Wyss wrote the book in German, the family was not named Robinson. The title of the novel *Der Schweizerische Robinson* actually translates to "The Swiss Robinson," implying that it is a Swiss "Robinson Crusoe" story. English publishers later gave the family the surname Robinson in order to capitalize on the use of resonance.

Settings

Interestingly, one hallmark of a bestseller is that it must transport the reader to another time and place. If you look at the bestselling movies and books of all time, every one of them takes the audience someplace special.

But the audience must want to be transported to that place. You have to find a "where and when" that people would like to go. Most people, for example, wouldn't want to go to a prison ship in 1744. A story about a young slave falling in love on such a ship wouldn't do well. The setting is heartbreaking.

So readers prefer to be transported to "sexy" settings, as the legendary agent Albert Zuckerman puts it in *Writing the Blockbuster Novel*. Thus we have romance readers who may like to read books set only in Ireland, or during the Civil War, or on faraway planets.

So romance writers may do well if they set their novels in, say, historic England in 1800, but the same story set in North Carolina in that very same year, using characters with the very same names, and even the same incidents and descriptions would be a flop.

Motifs

Many times the resonance in a tale is based upon only a certain motif—the use of dragons or ghosts or zombies.

Similarly, we have plotting elements that are often resonant—wars, heists, escapes, hunts, and so on.

Characters

Sometimes a character in a story will resonate with others that we have known and loved. Authors may try to resonate with famous fictional characters, such as a plucky teen like Pollyanna, or a miser like Scrooge.

I have known authors who will populate their novels with movie stars in an effort to create some resonance. Thus, a detective named Daniel Stark may look and speak just like Jack Nicholson. Or maybe a baseball player might look like Tom Cruise. Fans who recognize what the author is doing really find it delightful, since they can more easily imagine the characters. So authors may try to resonate with famous actors.

A similar thing happens when I as a writer do a movie tie-in. With my *Star Wars* novels, many young readers wrote fan letters telling me how well I had brought the characters to life. It was easy to do—after watching the movies a couple of dozen times.

Series writers will often use the same character as a detective over and over. Thus, if you loved Sherlock Holmes in one novel, you may be eager to read about him in another. The same principle applies to some other powerful adventure characters—Tarzan, Conan, James Bond and many others. In short, a novel or a series of novels may have what we call "internal resonance," where parts of the story resonate with the writer's own past works.

However, some types of books don't adapt well to a series. With romances, once a couple falls in love, you can't really re-tell their love story successfully. Having them break up and then get back together isn't as fun as the original story.

Shared Experience

As I mentioned earlier, sometimes the resonance in a novel comes from experiences that the author and purchaser have in common. Authors are often told to "Write what you know." If you've worked in the military, you can probably write well enough about it so that it will resonate with others who have shared your experiences. If you've gone through a divorce, you can touch other readers more easily, and so on.

Nostalgic experiences can be almost magical. The movie *A Christmas Story* worked well because it played upon experiences that many of us have lived through. I remember wanting a Red Ryder BB gun when I was a kid, and as a toddler, I had to wear a coat that would never let me put my arms down.

Weaving it all Together

Most of the time, in any given paragraph, you as an author load your work with so much resonance, touch so many strings of human experience, that it becomes difficult to untangle them all.

You may be writing about a character similar to heroes from other novels and set the story in an England as viewed through your own experiences visiting five years ago. In writing about a war, you might draw upon conflicts found in famous battles and upon your own experience in losing a friend in a war. You might use language that feels appropriate to the time and place, seeking out imagery from famous painting for inspiration.

The beauty of this is that you do it subconsciously. Your readers of course are almost always unaware of what you're doing, but you create a comfortable tale for your reader and create confidence in your abilities as a writer, by resonating with the rest of literature and with life in general.

A Case Study in Using Resonance: Tolkien

I'd like to show how one great writer wowed an audience using resonance. Let's use J.R.R. Tolkien as an example. Books and movies based on his works are widely popular, so you're probably familiar with them.

But there is another reason that I would like to use him as an example. A few years ago I was at a conference where a renowned writer dismissed Tolkien's work as a "literary trick." I've heard other critics occasionally take swipes at him, claiming that his work is juvenile and has little merit. Now, I'm not going to claim that he was the world's greatest stylist, and I can certainly see weaknesses in his writing, but I believe that such comments are . . . uninformed.

Often when we talk about a writer who is a great stylist, we say that he has "fine literary sensibilities." In other words, he recognizes what sounds beautiful and what does not, and so he brings his story to life with grace and power.

Of course by saying that, it suggests that *few* writers have fine sensibilities.

But the truth is that most of us have fine sensibilities in one area or another. Orson Scott Card has a phenomenal ear for dialogue.

Shannon Hale writes metaphors that leave me breathless. Brandon Sanderson has an unfailing sense of pacing. Steven King has been praised for being a modern Shakespeare when it comes to imitating the voice of the common man.

So most well-known authors have a major strength. With Tolkien, when it comes to an understanding of and the use of resonance, he may have had few equals in all of literature. He not only used resonance in all of the ways that I spoke about above—he discovered new methods that no one else had ever considered. His personal sensibilities were acutely focused on how a work resonated.

I read *Lord of the Rings* as a teenager and felt overwhelmed by its power and originality. Now I have to warn you that this article will be a spoiler, and by the time that you're done reading it, you may lose some respect for Tolkien's "originality."

I hope that you don't lose respect. Tolkien drew inspiration from not just hundreds, but thousands of sources, and it is beyond the scope of what I'm doing here to detail all of them. In fact, I'm sure that I would fail in any such attempt. I'm only trying to give you a sense for what he is doing, to scratch the surface of his work

Before I begin, it's important for you to know that Tolkien was a master philologist (lover of words), and his first civilian job after

WWI was to work on the *Oxford English Dictionary*, researching the roots of Germanic words. (For those who are not familiar with the *Oxford English Dictionary*, it is the most exhaustive of English dictionaries in that it discusses in detail, not only the meanings of words, but their history, usage, and etymology. When I talk about the *Oxford English Dictionary*, I am not referring to the condensed volume you sometimes see in stores. The last published *Oxford English Dictionary* was 20 volumes long.)

Echoing Other Works: Der Ring des Nibelung and The Lord of the Rings

The book "Lord of the Rings" echoes the title of Wagner's classic German opera *Der Ring des Nibelung*, which is best translated as "Nibelung's Ring." The two tales have some similarities. From Wikipedia, here is a brief synopsis of the opera:

> The plot revolves around a magic ring that grants the power to rule the world, forged by the Nibelung dwarf Alberich from gold he stole from the

Rhine maidens in the river Rhine. With the assistance of Loge, Wotan — the chief of the gods — steals the Ring from Alberich, but is forced to hand it over to the giants, Fafner and Fasolt. Wotan's schemes to regain the Ring, spanning generations, drive much of the action in the story. His grandson, the mortal Siegfried, wins the ring — as Wotan intended — but is eventually betrayed and slain as a result of the intrigues of Alberich's son Hagen. Finally, the Valkyrie Brünnhilde — Siegfried's lover and Wotan's estranged daughter — returns the ring to the Rhine maidens. In the process, the gods and their home, Valhalla, are destroyed.

Does it sound at all familiar? In *The Lord of the Rings,* the One Ring is forged of gold and gives the wielder the power to rule the world. The character of Wotan appears in LOTR in the guise of Gandalf. In both tales, the ringbearer is repeatedly referred to as the "Lord of the Ring." Many people struggle to gain the ring, and eventually, instead of casting it into a river (a plan that Frodo suggests), it is thrown into the Crack of Doom.

So plot-wise there are a number of similar elements between the two works. Upon reading *The Lord of the Rings*, one might be tempted to conclude that the One Ring is an allegory for the nuclear bomb. Both, it would seem, are an ultimate weapon. And Tolkien's use of a quest to destroy the Ring certainly mirrors many a person's desire to rid the world of this "ultimate weapon."

But Tolkien wasn't writing an allegory about the A-bomb—at least not consciously. He was familiar with war, having fought in WWI, and I'm sure that he knew that in every war, there is a new ultimate weapon, whether it be the fighter planes of WWI, or the underwater mines of the Crimean War—it is all the same. In the 1100s it was the trebuchet and the crossbow. Every war brings its new horrors, and the Ring that represented those horrors is based upon sources lost in antiquity.

While the story form itself was probably inspired by the opera (or by one of the German sagas that inspired the opera), both stories also share a lead character—the Norse god Odin (or Wotan), a god of wisdom, war, and travel. Odin of course is often depicted as a man robed for travel with a walking stick and a long gray beard, and among the Roman pantheon he is equated with the god Mercury.

There is no doubt that the two were one and the same god. There is also little doubt that Gandalf is modeled on Odin—a wise traveler who is also a master of war. In fact, here is the artist George von Rosen's 1886 depiction of Odin.

No one who has seen the movies or other representations of Gandalf can fail to recognize that he and Odin are one and the same. Yet sometimes even the author doesn't recognize the source of a character that he creates. For example, Tolkien once found an old postcard from Germany in his belongings and wrote on the back of it that the postcard—which showed an old wizard feeding a deer—served as inspiration for Gandalf.

But critics have shown that it couldn't have served as inspiration. Tolkien had actually created Gandalf several years *before* he saw the postcard. I suspect that instead, Rosen's picture of Odin, shown here, served as Tolkien's inspiration for Gandalf.

The similarities between the characters can be seen in the design of Gandalf—who is shown wearing Mercury's traditional gray traveling robe and peaked cap in the image below—from the film.

Resonance with Names

Years ago, a friend who owned a video game company called me and said, "Dave, I have a problem. We've made this great fantasy videogame, but we don't have a name for our hero. I've been going over names with my staff for days, and we're stuck. How do you name a fantasy character?"

"That's easy," I said. "You take two words that come to mind to describe that character, then put them together, and consider their sounds to make sure that they resonate properly."

I then asked him to describe the character in five or six words, and I spat out a name. My friend was silent for a moment, and then said, "That's perfect. That's perfect! We've been beating our heads against a wall for weeks, and you come up with the name in ten seconds. Tell me again how you do that?"

I can't even recall the name, but I met the friend a few weeks ago, and he reminded me of the incident. So I'll try to make this process a little clearer.

A classic example of this might be seen in George Lucas's use of the name Darth Vader. "Darth" is probably a contraction of "dark" and "death," or it might be a modification of "dearth." "Vader" could be a truncation of "invader," or it could simply be Dutch (vader) for "father." Hence, I'm fairly certain that it is inspired by the words "dark," "death," "invader" and "father." But by happy coincidence, it resonates with other dire-sounding words as well.

Similarly, Tolkien used these techniques in creating names. Some of his names are easily untangled. Treebeard is an ancient tree with a lichen-like beard. Mount Doom doesn't need to be untangled at all. Mordor, the name of the evil kingdom where Sauron dwells, sounds like "murder," but of course "more" and "door," the two words that make up the name, suggest that by entering this place, you might be walking through a door into murder.

However, Tolkien complicates what Lucas did by using names that often have foreign roots. Remember that Tolkien was a philologist, one of the world's foremost authorities on the origins of words with Germanic roots. He was very familiar with old German, Norse, Danish, English, and so on.

Take Gandalf Greyhame. The name "Gandalf" is an Old Norse name taken from a list of dwarves from folklore. The word Gandalf is a contraction of gandr (wand) and alf (elf). Hence his name literally means "elf with a wand." But you don't have to speak Old Norse for it to resonate. In English it sounds like a contraction of grand and elf. So whether you are talking Old Norse or English, the sound of the name resonates. Greyhame is a bit easier. Hame is an Old Dutch word for "home," and is also the root for the word "hamlet." Thus, the name itself sounds like "gray home," (much like the Gray Havens that the Elves in The Lord of the Rings are fleeing to for refuge). Tolkien says that the word translates into one of his mythical languages as "gray mantle"—which is an odd mistake for Tolkien to make. Having words in two separate languages that are spoken as "gray" and that mean "gray" sounds odd. It just doesn't happen unless those languages are linked by common roots. Tolkien once lamented that the name Gandalf was concocted unwisely in an hour with little thought, but it's still quite serviceable as a name.

Here's another name: Gollum. Gollum is a hobbit-like character who was magically turned by sorcerous power into a monster. His name is obviously morphed from the word "golem," which in Jewish folklore was a creature made from inanimate materials—such as twigs and string—so that it was magically transformed into a living servant. In many ways, Gollum is a golem—a monster given long life so that he can serve his evil master.

What about the name Sauron? Once again, Tolkien says that it has a meaning in a foreign tongue (the elvish language Quenya) and that it means "abhorred." But the name has entirely different roots. In Greek, the word saur means "lizard," as in "dino-saur." The suffix on in "Sauron" means "the first." Hence, Sauron's name translated from Greek is "The First Lizard," or perhaps more appropriately, "The Great Lizard" or even "The Lizard King." Tolkien would have known this. So Sauron is, in essence, the king of all cold-hearted creatures, the ultimate heartless killer.

Interestingly, Tolkien seemed to be keyed into creating names as a way of developing his characters.

I've seen poets—Leslie Norris, Shakespeare, and Tennyson—who seem to be led by sounds to create stories. An internal rhyme may suggest a couple of words, which then lead to a sentence. The sentence gives rise to a paragraph in which an interesting string of words creates a whole new image that must be elaborated upon—which leads to a new twist in the plot of the tale.

So for some authors, sound leads to story. For Tolkien, a name like Gollum suggests both a backstory and an ending.

But Tolkien was more keyed into his characterization by resonance than most. For example, early in The Lord of the Rings he had a character that Frodo met at an inn—a dangerous character nicknamed Trotter because of the clattering sound that his wooden shoes made when he walked over cobblestones. But editors warned Tolkien that the character sounded silly.

So Tolkien turned Trotter into Strider—a character who became rather regal. "Strider" of course has its roots in "strident," which suggests that this is not only a person who travels, but one who does so with a deadly purpose. Later, even that name did not suffice. Strider was in fact a man on a mission to reestablish himself as a rightful king—so Tolkien lets us know that Strider's real name was "Aragorn," a name that has interesting resonance. (Aragon is the name of a royal family in Spain, which suggested a whole plot line)

One reader, Ami Chopine, said, "I searched Aragorn, recalling Catherine of Aragon who had first married Henry VIII. Came up with all sorts of interesting things, such as the Drown of Aragon which was the uniting of several kingdoms in Spain and Western Europe. Geographically speaking, in Europe, Spain approximately resembles where Gondor is in Middle-earth, and the Kingdom of Aragon itself is about where the city of Gondor was.

"But then I did look into *arrogani*, and found that it comes through Old French and means 'claiming for oneself.'"

Consider the following plays on the name:
Aragorn
Era Gone (The story of *The Lord of the Rings* is one long lament at the end of the era of the Elves.)
Eragon (Tolkien isn't the only one who uses resonance!)

But of course we have that troubling "orn" sound on Aragorn, and we have a lot of words with the *orn* sound: born, morn, mourn, torn, and worn all come to mind.

Often, Tolkien's character or place names give hints to his societies. For example, the Dwarves often have names taken from Old Norse. Tolkien names one Dwarf Thorin Oakenshield—the name of an early Norse conqueror who settled in England.

In other words, the Dwarves symbolically represent the Norse in English history. The Elves, I suspect, have a language drawn from Gaellic, and represent the older inhabitants of England. Tolkien's Men represent the chivalric knights of the middle ages. Older creatures— ghosts, ancient woodsmen, and even trees, all serve as symbols of the land's past. In short, all of his ancient peoples are fighting to combat the future. But what future are they combating? Sauron's name is taken from Latin. I suspect that Tolkien was writing a tale in which all of England's past is fighting a New Rome, the next world order.

One young critic recently decried Tolkien's use of mishmash of styles in *Lord of the Rings* and said that he felt it didn't quite work. It's true that his style changes as he moves from dealing with Hobbits in one section, to Elves in another, to Men in a third, to Dwarves in a fourth, and so on.

Tolkien adapted the language in each section in order to evoke the proper period of English history.

Among Elves, the *el* is a common suffix or prefix—*El*rond, Tinuvi*el*. *El* of course is an old Hebrew word for "god," and thus his elves are given names that associate them with immortals. Tolkien once wrote a treatise on how the name "elf" has its roots in the Hebrew word "angel." The word "angel" is a compound of "messenger" and "god." The word "elf" literally has the same meaning. Hence, when Tolkien wrote of elves, he did not make them the little gnomish people that we associate with Santa, but instead made them creatures of light with almost divine powers, a little higher than us mere mortals.

So here is what you need to recognize about Tolkien's use of resonance in naming: on a linguistic level, he is looking at the roots of words and realizing how they affect his readers on a subconscious level. This way, when you read about a character named Elrond or Gandalf or Strider or Gollum or Sauron, you may know very little about that character, and yet somehow there is a sense of "rightness" about that character, a sense that he is more than he seems.

Resonating with Other Works

I discussed how Tolkien's The Lord of the Rings resonated with Wagner's operas. It also resonated with the poetry of Yeats and Tennyson along with the work of Shakespeare.

For example, in Macbeth, Malcom's soldiers disguise themselves with boughs in Birnam Wood and then march to Dunsinane hill. This part of the play inspired Tolkien to create his Ents—trees that actually move. In a letter he wrote to poet W.H. Auden, Tolkien said that after studying Macbeth he "longed" to create trees that really marched to war.

Also in the play, the witches prophesy that no man born of a woman can overpower Macbeth, but because Macduff was born by C-section, he manages to defeat Macbeth. This resonates with a similar situation in The Lord of the Rings. The Elf Glorfindel prophesies that the Witch-King cannot fall by a man, but Eowyn, a woman, slays the Witch-King.

Of course, Tolkien wasn't just trying to resonate with Shakespeare. He drew on other sources, some of them that were quite modern. Tolkien wrote The Lord of the Rings over a period of about 13 years, and he writes that in 1939 he ground to a halt at Balin's tomb. He says that it was "over a year later, in 1941 that I moved on . . ." Now, Fantasia was released in

1940, and I doubt that you will have to think about it long before you recognize the resemblance that the Balrog in The Lord of the Rings has to the demon from "Night on Bald Mountain" in Fantasia. It wasn't until Tolkien incorporated the demon Chernabog and wrote of the death of Gandalf that he was able to move forward. Here is Chernabog in picture form, followed by the Balrog.

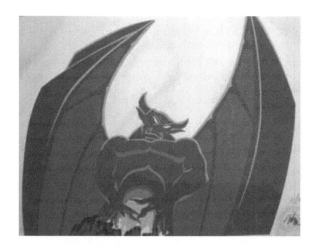

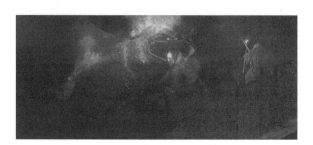

When I first read about the Balrog as a teen, I found it easy to envision him. Why? Because I'd seen him before. Even though I didn't make a conscious connection, I was familiar with the balrog from childhood, just as other images from the novels came with similar force.

Tolkien drew plenty of inspiration from Pre-Raphaelite artists. Notice the similarities between their work and his *Lord of the Rings*.

"Godspeed" by Edmund Blair Leighton

Note the borrowed dress design used
in *The Lord of the Rings*

"Ophelia" by John William
Waterhouse

Another costume used in *The Lord of the Rings*

"Oh What's that in the Hollow" by
Edward Robert Hughes

Resonant image from *The Lord of the Rings*

The point that I want to make here is this: Tolkien was not content to simply draw inspiration from high-brow operas. He took it from some of the most famous poets of his time, from ancient legends, from animated films, from great painters, and even from children's books, such as *Wind in the Willows*. (Compare "mad" Bilbo Baggins' journey from his underground home with that of Mole from *Wind in the Willows*. If you look closely, you'll see some interesting similarities.)

In short, Tolkien was like a sponge, seeking to draw resonance from tens of thousands of sources, and in doing so, create his own work that grew in strength and power.

That's how I suggest you try to imbue your work with resonance.

Resonating with Universal Experiences

There are other ways to gain resonance in your work than to simply draw from other works of art, or to listen closely to the sounds of the names that you create.

A third way to use resonance is to discuss experiences that are fairly universal. Tolkien does this as well. At one point, as Frodo prepares to leave the Shire, he stops and thinks about how this is a grand step in his life.

Who hasn't done the same? I remember my first day of school, at age six, thinking about how important a step it was in life. Again when I left high school and left home, I was much like Frodo, taking one long, last look at my house before I drove away. Anyone who has gone to college or to fight a war understands how keen that emotion can be.

Similarly, Tolkien reminds us of plenty of other moments that each of us has felt in life. When reading of Frodo and Sam creeping into Mordor, you might recall Frodo peering up and seeing a star. Smitten by the beauty of it, Frodo suddenly takes heart and marches forward boldly. Who hasn't felt inspired by the beauty and grandeur of nature?

Or when Gandalf falls into the crevasse—who hasn't ached with grief when a mentor is suddenly stripped away? Tolkien had to have seen good men "fall" in combat during WWI, and I believe that when he wrote that scene, he was trying to dramatize for us how this all-too-common emotion feels.

So Tolkien touches us with wonder one moment when we meet the elves, or with delight as his Hobbits get a fine meal of mushrooms from a local farmer, or relief when Gandalf finally realizes the secret of how to open an ancient door into a mountain. He reminds us of the love we might have felt for a good animal one moment, and a longing to be home another. At every turn, we are reminded by the Hobbits of how frightening and dangerous larger people can be, an emotion that is overwhelming for children at times.

That's one of the keys to drawing and holding an audience—creating scenes that resonate with readers emotionally, that touch them deeply because they themselves have lived through a similar experience.

A similar thing can be done with themes. One great editor, Sol Stein, mentioned that by simply touching upon a universal truth, we as authors can create a bond with our reader. Thus, when Tolkien writes about the corrupting influence of the One Ring, it's something that we all connect with. Tolkien was undoubtedly familiar with Lord Acton's quote, "Power corrupts, and absolute power corrupts absolutely." Tolkien's dramatization of that theme is outstanding.

There are a number of other ways to write an epic, though, to try capture a picture of life. The Russian critic argued that in order to write an epic, to give readers the illusion that a book captured the whole life, the author had to use all of the various levels of language of his society. This makes sense in Russian, where a commoner, a merchant, and a lord had vastly different dialects, and one can see a master at this technique in a modern fantasy writer, Patrick Rothfuss, in his epic masterpiece *The Name of the Wind*.

This concept is similar to Chaucer's belief that by writing about people in various occupations—lord, knight, merchant, serf—he could try to capture all of life. After all, nothing marks a person's class as much as his language.

Other critics have sought to cover the various stages of life in order to create an epic—childhood, young love, courtship, the raising of a family, old age and death.

Certainly Tolkien uses each of these techniques to some degree. But more importantly, I believe that Tolkien was trying to capture a world of *emotions* in order to give his work epic scope.

For those of you who want to write epics, you might want to take note of what he did.

But there is another way that you can create resonance in your story—through resonance within the work itself, or "internal" resonance.

Internal Resonance

Internal resonance occurs when a writer sets up a motif to a story, and deepens the readers' emotions by playing upon that motif. Let's discuss a couple of examples from Tolkien.

Writing Tip:

In creating a plot for a novel, we often expand upon a motif to create scenes. For example, in a "chase story," we may have a character seeking to elude capture, such as in the movie *The Fugitive*. Each capture attempt becomes more involved and more likely to succeed. So as a writer, when plotting the novel, we simply know that the next major try/fail cycle in the story will revolve around and attempted capture, an attempt that deepens and broadens the conflict.

Note that in discussing the three motifs that I pulled from Tolkien's work here, we see something similar. Tolkien writes a story about loss by having Frodo face loss again and again, each time in circumstances that are more and more distressing.

The technique is easy to master, and can add tremendous power to your story.

The Lord of the Rings is a story of loss, a tale of how each of us experiences the wonders and the beauties of the world, and then must leave them behind. Tolkien begins setting us up for this loss right from the beginning. Frodo Baggins is hesitant to leave the Shire when he was supposed to, for he doesn't really want to lose his home, Bag End. Yet he puts it up for sale and makes a big show of leaving, spending many a night to walk its trails in the starlight and say his goodbyes. This almost does him in, for he is nearly captured by the Nine Dark Riders.

Yet he finds refuge from them in the home of Farmer Maggot, and reluctantly says goodbye to a new-found friend.

Then again, the same type of action is repeated in the home of Tom Bombadil.

And once again he finds solace and friendship in Rivendell, and is forced to leave.

Frodo then finds friendship among his traveling companions, but Gandalf is torn from the party in the Mines of Moria, and once again Frodo is forced to flee with his life in danger.

In Lothlorien Frodo takes refuge, and like a man who has been jilted by his lover, he offers his ring to Galadriel. But all too soon he realizes that in order to keep her safe, he has to leave Lothlorien.

Indeed, he decides to leave everyone behind at the end of *The Fellowship* of the Ring, and races off even as the Orcs attack his friends.

Do you see what Tolkien is doing? At least seven times in one novel, Frodo is forced to escape from places of comfort and refuge. And he leaves behind his refuge a couple more times in the succeeding novels.

Tolkien is of course setting us up for the very end of the novel, that moment where Frodo must sail off into the Grey Havens, leaving behind the world that he loved so dearly, the world that he saved.

Had Tolkien not emphasized how much Frodo (an orphan) longed for a home, that final scene would have had very little impact indeed. Instead, Frodo's final farewell to the Shire is devastating, a real tear-jerker.

But do you see how Tolkien did it? He simply repeated an action over and over again, playing upon variations, trying to make each instance of leaving more powerful and difficult than the last—when appropriate.

Here's another example, a very simple but powerful one. Perhaps one of the most compelling scenes for me was the Fellowship's journey into and through the mines of Moria.

Do you recall the opening to that scene? The group must walk along the edge of a still pool, where the only sound is the occasional sound of dripping water. The very solitude of the place sets them all on edge. One of the Hobbits throws a rock, and moments later the group is attacked by the "watcher" of the lake.

They escape the monster and make it into the Mines of Moria, only to have the door blocked with boulders behind them.

Inside the mine, Frodo cannot sleep that night for the dripping sound of water. (Note the repetition of a single spooky element, made unsettling by the attack of the watcher.) A few nights later, that dripping sound is replaced by the distant sound of a hammer going, tink, tink, clank, tink.

Suddenly, Frodo realizes that he's not alone, and soon he sees the glowing eyes of Gollum in the cave.

Finally, as they near the exit, the "plink" of water, the "tink" of a hammer, is suddenly replaced by the sound of drums in the deep—huge thunderous sounds that roll through the cavern, roaring "Doom! Doom! Doom!"

Here, the internal resonance is simply a repeated sound, one that grows louder, more unsettling, and more menacing with each repetition.

Here's a third use of internal resonance in *The Lord of the Rings*: the journey through the underworld. We see the first hint of it in the Shire, when the Hobbits escape one of the nine riders by diving off the road. They find themselves in a cave-like overhang while one of the nine riders tries to draw them out, and

Frodo imagines himself suddenly to be in a tunnel.

Later, as they leave the Shire, they dive through a hcdgc—and find themselves in a forest so deep that it seems almost lightless. After leaving Tom Bombadil's house, they take too long on the road, and find themselves suddenly dragged into the lightless burrow of a wight.

They find themselves in another tunnel at the inn at Bree—a hobbit hole, where once again they are attacked by the nine riders.

They make it to Weathertop, and Frodo is stabbed with a magic blade that breaks off— but begins working its way to his heart. As he loses consciousness, he once again imagines himself to be in a tunnel.

The group heads toward Mordor, and along the way our protagonists are forced to take an ill-fated detour through the Mines of Moria.

Frodo and Sam later split off from the group and make their journey to Mordor— having to take Gollum's secret path that will lead through Shelob's lair.

Merry and Pippin mirror that journey as they journey into the Entwood, beneath trees so old and hoary that they block out all light— until Merry and Pippin find themselves given shelter in Treebeard's cave.

Gandalf himself has a lightless journey after falling into the pit in the Mines of Moria.

There, he chases the Balrog through endless caverns in an epic duel that is only related as he tells it to the Hobbits.

Meanwhile, Aragorn and the others take their own lightless journeys—fighting the orcs in the caverns at Helm's Deep— until at last Aragorn must take one final journey through a tunnel so that he can summon the spirits of the dead to fight in behalf of Gondor.

And we cannot forget the final lightless journey—Frodo's journey to the Crack of Doom.

Each of these lightless journeys, of course, is a play upon a theme, designed to heighten that final moment when Frodo steps toward the Crack of Doom—and all light fails him.

So, there I've given you three examples of how Tolkien uses internal resonance in *The Lord of the Rings* in order to heighten his reader's emotions. Perhaps you will find this tool of some value as you plot your own novels.

Language in The Lord of the Rings

In 1962, Anthony Burgess published *A Clockwork Orange*, a futuristic morality tale dealing with the futility of using aversion therapy in trying to rehabilitate criminals. Critics have often praised the work for being bold and imaginative—in particular because Burgess creates his own slang. It seems that at the time, the idea that our language would evolve in the future and that a writer took that into account was something of a literary breakthrough.

Yet Tolkien did something far more involved than come up with half a dozen neologisms and a couple of shifts in syntax. Tolkien began to play with languages in a way that few have ever done, and all of this deals with resonance. So it bothers me when I hear modern writers refer to what Tolkien did as a "literary stunt," while many of those same folks would hail Anthony Burgess as a genius.

Let me see if I can explain what Tolkien did. Right now I am writing in English. It's a rather large language, primarily because it borrows from so many other languages. Throughout history, England has been conquered by a number of peoples—the Danes, the Normans, the Norse, the Anglo-Saxons, the Romans, and so on. With each invasion, the nobility and even some of the commoners adopted the language of the conquerors, so that often when we speak, we have a choice of several different words to choose from, each borrowed from a separate tongue, that all have roughly the same meaning.

But of course, we don't need words to mean the same, so we assign slightly different definitions to the words—we give them nuances. Thus, as the sun falls behind the hills we might say that it is "evening," "twilight," "dusk," "gloaming," "sunset," or "nightfall." In each of our minds, we develop a sense of gradations that probably don't exist in most other languages. In my mind, evening is brighter than gloaming. Twilight is right in the middle of the act. Sunset is the moment when the sun is gone from the sky, and so on.

Added to this barrage of conquerors, England sometimes became home to various refugees—such as Gypsies, Moors, and Jews—and England was also visited by traders and missionaries from other nations, so that the language absorbed terms this way.

Then of course, as the English empire spread across the world, people came in contact with dozens of other cultures throughout Asia, Africa, Australia and the Americas, and when a word was found that was useful, that word fell into common usage in English. Thus we have words like "desert," which was borrowed from the Arabs. The English language didn't require such a term— there are no deserts in England.

The result is that today there are over two million words in the English language by some estimates, when you take into account all of the various terms used in specialized trades like law, medicine, the sciences, and so on.

By contrast, most cultures get by with far fewer words. If you are living in a village in the Pacific islands where your society has had no contact with the outside world, you don't need a huge vocabulary. You don't need words like "engine," "printing press," or "processors." Some languages have fewer than ten thousand words total. Often, new words are created in such languages by simply stacking existing nouns. A fellow once told me that in one Asian country where he lived, the word for white man was, "pigs that walk on two feet and talk, ha, ha!"

So English has absorbed a large number of languages, and of course linguists realized long ago that words from different cultures tend to have various effects upon us emotionally. A person who uses a large number of Latinate words while speaking is often considered to be something of an egghead. A person who uses French too much may seem pretentious. Words from Old Dutch or Old Norse are often considered crude.

As a philologist, Tolkien noted the influence that such words had upon his readers. As he began writing *The Lord of the Rings*, he realized that his Hobbits, his Men, his Elves, Orcs, Trolls, Dwarves, and so on would all need to have their own languages. Since, according to old German legend, the Elves and Dwarves were both offshoots of the same race, he initially decided to create languages for them that had Old German and Old Norse roots, while his Hobbits spoke a language with Old English roots.

Like many linguists, Tolkien surely became enamored with trying to imagine what the precursor language to all of these tongues might have been. It is obvious as you look at them that they seem to have a single source, that Old Danish, Norse, English and a dozen other languages were all branches from one tree, sharing a common root. (Go to a copy of the *Oxford English Dictionary* and just thumb through at random if you like. You'll find many words like "home" or "father" that have citations in a dozen languages that sound very similar, with only slight vowel shifts or the dropping of a consonant to differentiate them.)

So Tolkien was enamored with these common roots, and he created his tongue "Westron" that was spoken by Hobbits and Dwarves. He modified his language so that it would seem to be a "precursor" to modern Germanic languages. Then he went back in time and developed a precursors and offshoots of Westron, much as I'm sure that he felt such languages might have developed. Tolkien took his development of races and cultures to an almost unimaginable extreme.

Sadly, if you look at his Elves and Dwarves as characters alone, they seem to lack some personality. Instead, they seem more to be rather stock representations of their kind. So he differentiated their kinds.

The goal of course was to create races that felt real—that resonated with his readers. Often, he did so by rooting his invented languages in sounds of languages drawn from our distant past.

Now, on something of a side note, if you look at Tolkien's work, it becomes clear that his works were written with poetic effects in mind.

Let's take a sample, a simple descriptive passage chosen at random. Gandalf is riding beside Legolas, Gimli, and Aragorn, when he sees a city from afar and asks the Elf to describe what he sees in the distance:

> Legolas gazed ahead, shading
> his eyes from the level shafts of
> the new-risen sun. 'I see a
> white stream that comes down
> from the snows,' he said.
> 'Where it issues from the
> shadow of the vale a green hill
> rises upon the east. A dike and
> mighty wall and thorny fence
> encircle it. Within there rise the
> roofs of houses; and in the
> midst, set upon a green terrace,
> there stands aloft a great hall of
> Men. And it seems to my eyes

that it is thatched with gold.
The light of it shines far over
the land. Golden, too, are the
posts of its doors. There men
in bright mail stand; but all else
within the courts are asleep.'

'Edoras those courts are called,'
said Gandalf, 'and Meduseld is
the golden hall. There dwells
Theoden son of Thengel, King
of the Mark of Rohan. . . .'

Now, as you look at these lines, you'll
note a lot of poetic effects. First, look at the
cadence. The length of the sentences seems
very similar at first, but with each line the word
count winds down:

Legolas gazed ahead, shading his eyes
from the level shafts of the new-risen
sun.
'I see a white stream that comes down
from the snows,' he said.
'Where it issues from the shadow of
the vale a green hill rises upon the east.
A dike and mighty wall and thorny
fence encircle it.
Within there rise the roofs of houses;
and in the midst,

set upon a green terrace, there stands
aloft a great hall of Men.
And it seems to my eyes that it is
thatched with gold.
The light of it shines far over the land.
Golden, too, are the posts of its doors.
There men in bright mail stand;
but all else within the courts are
asleep.'

'Edoras those courts are called,' said
Gandalf,
'and Meduseld is the golden hall.
There dwells Theoden son of Thengel,
King of the Mark of Rohan. . . .'

It seems to me that Tolkien wrote these
lines to be read aloud, or perhaps chanted, as
ancient storytellers would have done. As
Hemingway once said, "The secret to all great
writing is that it is poetry."

If you don't see the poetry in the
language, study the use of assonance. For
example, notice how the long-I sound is
repeated in the first two lines, or the long-O
sound that runs throughout the passage, tying
it together, and look at how consonance is
used in his sentences, especially in the midst of
each line. Such things are common in well
written tales.

But note too, how it is loaded with archaic language, words whose meanings have fallen out of use in the past four hundred years: vale, midst, aloft, hall, thatched, mail, courts, dwells, Mark. (Note that in this instance, the word "mark" may have one of two archaic meanings behind it. A "mark" is a tract of land upon the frontier, which describes Theoden's realm well. But the word "mark" also describes any tract of land owned communally by German peasants.)

But what interests me so much isn't Tolkien's rather common use of poetic devices: it's what happens when he begins creating names and languages. When he mentions the names Edoras, Meduseld, Theoden, Thengel, and Mark of Rohan—there is something exciting about his language, a sense that it sounds familiar and if you studied it sufficiently, you just might figure out where it came from.

I mentioned that he used Germanic languages in creating much of this, but Tolkien went much further than creating just one language. He also developed languages for his various elven races, for Orcs, for the Dark Lord Sauron, and so on.

Now, just how many "languages" Tolkien created is hard to know. He names twenty or thirty in his works, but naming a language and creating a fully functioning lexicon are not quite the same things. What Tolkien really did,

I suspect, is create three or four languages, and then try to show how they would have evolved over time as new dialects arose and then morphed over the ages into entirely different languages. So listing thirty names for languages doesn't mean that he had created full lexicons for each of them.

The important thing to note here, I think, is that Tolkien began to experiment with languages in some interesting ways. Some of Tolkien's invented languages are rooted in our own. Thus his humans and his dwarves are given names that resonate with us. But among his elves, he does something different. Tolkien begins by trying to create a new language—a more elegant, musical, and beautiful language—than has ever existed before, a language of perfect poetry. Then for his Orcs, he creates a language that is more harsh and dissonant than others—a sinister and brutal language of grunts and hisses—that has interesting similarities to his elvish tongue.

As Tolkien began creating his languages, about mid-way through *The Lord of the Rings* his work takes on new dimensions. You can go to various lands—the Shire, Rohan, Gondor, Lothlorien—and you'll find that entire passages of description suddenly shift in style depending upon the land that you're visiting.

Years ago, when I wrote my first novel, *On My Way to Paradise*, I was dealing with a Panamanian doctor. In order to get it to sound natural, I often had to write most of the dialogue in Spanish, and then translate it into English.

Tolkien was doing the same kind of thing, to a degree, with Old Norse, Old English, and so on. As a linguist, Tolkien became so attuned to words, that when he wrote, he began to try to create resonance through his choice of *cenemes*—the smallest units of language. That's what separates him from the vast majority of writers, and that's why even thirty-five years after I first picked up and enjoyed his work, I still respect what he did. Tolkien is definitely not a one-trick pony, a hack, or a fraud—as some modern critics might assert.

Let me explain in more depth, since I'm sure that most of my readers haven't studied linguistics. Normally when we talk about speech, we divide it into "phonemes," small units of sound. We say that English, for example, has about 40 phonemes. Those phonemes are considered to be basic units of sound. Each of our consonants is a phoneme, as are a number of combinations—st, fr, th, gr, ch, wh, and so on. Then of course we have our vowels, which each have long sounds, short sounds, and various other forms, and we have semi-vowels like y and w that have a couple of possibilities.

If you look at another language, say Navajo, you'll find that it is built from a different set of phonemes, many of which are practically unpronounceable to native English speakers.

Then of course you can go to the click languages of Africa, and to whistling languages of certain South American Indians, which use sounds that aren't spoken in the traditional way at all, and you have new sets of "phonemes."

The problem of course for a linguist like Tolkien is that he recognizes that languages aren't really made of phonemes any more than matter is made of atoms. There is a smaller unit of sound—the ceneme—from which languages are composed. The cenemes can be subtly different from the phonemes. For example, the "st" in "fist" is subtly different both in sound and pronunciation from the "st" in "strong." If you say both sounds, you'll notice that in "fist" you put more emphasis on the "t." In "strong" you emphasize the "s."

As a linguist seeking the roots of words, Tolkien had to become adept at listening to cenemes for clues to a word's origination rather than the larger, clumsier phoneme.

And of course in trying to create his own languages, this became very important. He had to pay attention to even these smallest units of sound when creating his languages.

Tolkien went back and did something quite amusing linguistically. One of his conceits for his world was that Elves, Gnomes, Orcs, Dwarves, and such were all real, and that their languages—and our language—all evolved from a common tongue spoken by the first elves.

So Tolkien had to deal with language creation at the smallest possible unit—the ceneme.

To try to create a unified language that takes into account all other languages is something that a couple of linguists have idly talked about doing, but no one that I know of besides Tolkien has really tried it. How would you account for click languages, and so on?

To tell the truth, I understand Tolkien's impulse. If you've been to England, particularly the area where he was born and raised, every hill, every trail, every old stack of bricks has a name. The name might be an Old English name, a Latin name, a Welsh name, a Norse name, and so on. Of course many of the towns have names that were once spoken in Latin, but got changed by the Welsh, and then became pronounced differently by the English, etc. So names of things in his area can be very confusing, and when you hear a name, if you're a word lover, you just have to try to make sense of it.

In the same way, Tolkien became interested in trying to make sense of language as a whole. Sure, he knew that he couldn't reconstruct it. But he found joy in playing with it.

So Tolkien was exploring language in a way that no writer before or since has ever done. He focused on it even to the level of the ceneme.

In Conclusion

As a writer, Tolkien was keenly interested in using resonance both to inspire his creation and to ensnare an audience. In his exploration of language, he went deeper than any author before him.

I feel almost as if he is an explorer who went to a distant land and returned with great treasures.

Of course, there are certainly many people who aren't interested in using resonance on that level. You probably won't spend the rest of your life learning ancient languages so that you can duplicate Tolkien's effects. But at the same time, I find what he did to be both intriguing and enlightening.

Resonance within a Genre

Earlier I discussed how authors use resonance within a genre. For many pages now, I've been discussing Tolkien. I recall as a teen feeling that his works were unique and original, yet somehow haunting. I wasn't familiar then with many of the precursors to Tolkien's works.

It may not be obvious to a new writer, but resonance is the single greatest draw that you can try to invest into your work. When most people choose to buy a book or go to a movie, it is because it resonates with things that they have seen and enjoyed before.

A couple of years ago, I went out to sell books at the fair. I had dozens of books on display, and some of them have been around for years, but this was the first time that I'd ever been able to sit in front of buyers and get their reactions to the books. Frequently I had teens grab a Runelords book and say, "Oh, this is what dad likes." Sometimes they even knew which book he'd read, but many of them would then look at the books a bit confusedly and then say, "Oh, no, this just looks like them." Invariably the dad was either a reader of Terry Brooks or Robert Jordan, and the teen had simply recognized the style of the cover art. Yet in most cases, after realizing that I wasn't Brooks or Jordan, the wife would pick up one of my books anyway. Why? Resonance. My book looked like the kind that her husband might like.

In other cases, moms would grab book five in the series and say, "Has Jaden read this one yet?" The book pictures a young man on a graak, a dragon-like creature; it turns out that there are a lot of Jadens out there who only like to read books about dragons. Once again, resonance.

If you ask a person who describes himself as a "big science fiction and fantasy fan" what he likes to read, you will almost always find that his tastes are rather narrow. They'll tell you, "I like J.K. Rowling" or "I love Orson Scott Card." In short, they have a favorite author in the genre but haven't read beyond that author. Or maybe they've read widely in a certain franchise—Dragonlance or Star Wars. Resonance.

So the question in my mind is, just how many people buy books because they resonate with other works, and how many actually buy for novelty?

Take a look at the fantasy and science fiction market. The fantasy market is much larger than the science fiction market. I can't say how much larger for sure, but years ago I was told by industry professionals that fantasy appeared to be outselling science fiction by about six to one. In the years since, science fiction sales have dropped dramatically. I suspect that fantasy outsells science fiction by more than ten to one.

But forty years ago there was no "fantasy" market. There was no section in the bookstores that said "fantasy" anywhere. Tolkien's *The Lord of the Rings* became something of a cult hit in the 1960s and grew into the 1970s. It wasn't until 1977, when Terry Brooks came out with *The Sword of Shannara* that a fantasy novel hit *The New York Times* Bestseller list, and Brooks stayed on top of the list for five months. That is when fantasy as a "genre" was born.

Sure, there had been fantasy novels before. Robert E. Howard's Conan stories began appearing in the early 1930s, along with the work of Fritz Lieber and others, and these surely had an influence on Tolkien. But most of those early works were printed in magazines, and there were not sections yet devoted to the "fantasy" genre.

But once Terry Brooks hit the big time, publishers began to respond to a perceived demand for fantasy.

Of course a lot of things got shelved with the fantasy, but the most commercially successful works were those that best imitated Tolkien. These are usually stories set in 1) a medieval setting, 2) with a small cast of people traveling on a quest, 3) in a world populated by several species of intelligent humanoids, including wizards, and so on.

Examples of this include works by Brooks, Jordan, Weiss and Hickman, etc.— who have been, by the way, the most commercially successful writers in the fantasy genre until just recently.

One quote, from *The New York Times*, on Robert Jordan's novels says "Jordan has come to dominate the world Tolkien began to reveal." And that is true. Of the fantasy writers of the past 15 years, Jordan has been most successful, selling literally millions of copies. But if you look closely at the first hundred pages of *Eye of the World*, you will see dozens (even hundreds, if you want to get nit-picky) of parallels between Jordan's work and Tolkien's.

The parallels start when you open the book. Before each story begins, we see a map. Tolkien's map shows his world, Middle-earth, "at the end of the third age." Jordan's novel has a map with a strikingly similar coast line, and at the end of Jordan's brief and powerful prologue, we see that he quotes historians from "the Fourth Age." There are other similarities in the maps. Tolkien has his Mount Doom, while Jordan has his Mountains of Dhoom. Tolkien talks of his Misty Mountains, Jordan has (on his second map) the Mountains of Mist.

In both novels, we begin with a celebration. In *The Lord of the Rings*, Tolkien's

Hobbits plan to celebrate a birthday party. Jordan's characters plan to celebrate Bel Tine.

In *The Lord of the Rings*, the wizard Gandalf plans to make an unusual appearance and sets off fireworks. In Jordan's novel, wizards make an unusual appearance in town and thus add to the spectacle of the planned fireworks.

In *The Lord of the Rings*, our hero is a young man, a rustic gentleman farmer, who barely escapes his home with three companions when the Dark Riders begin their hunt. With Jordan, our hero is a young man, a poor farmer, who barely escapes his home with three companions when trollocs attack. (Note that in Tolkien's world we have trolls, in Jordan's we have trollocs.)

Now, I could go on for pages like this, dissecting sentences to show how Jordan is establishing resonance with Tolkien, Howard, Arthurian legend, and so on. Yet I feel like I've done enough of that. Rather, I'd like to get to the point of what I'm trying to say: Robert Jordan is a very fine and powerful writer in his own right. He could have created his own fantasy world, populated it with creatures from his own imagination, and given us something new. But he recognized that there was a vast audience out there who was still looking for something that resonated deeply with Tolkien's work, and he made the choice to capture that existing audience rather than write in the hope that he might gather his own fans independently.

The truth is that if you write something startlingly original, it is very difficult to sell. Tolkien's *The Lord of the Rings* went to dozens of publishers before it found a home, yet now if you look at most polls by fantasy readers, it is considered the greatest fantasy of all time.

Similarly, in science fiction, the novel *Dune* is now considered by most readers to be the best Science Fiction novel ever written— but Frank Herbert went through every publisher in New York before a magazine company decided to give it a shot.

If you try to create and sell a truly original fantasy, publishers won't know what to do with it. So let's say you write about creatures that you call "Golunds." Your protagonist has three legs and two heads. He lives in a land called Neuropa, and his great conflict is that he hopes to find love in a land where all solicitations for affection are outlawed. You send your masterpiece into a publisher and manage to hook an editor. They love it. "What shelf should we put it on?" they'll ask. "How do we market it? What other bestseller is it most like?" If you answer, "It's totally different!" they will not be happy. In fact, it will never make it past the marketing board.

So as a writer, you need to consider, "What other works will my book resonate with?"

One way to do this is to aim a book right down the reader's throat. Look at the age of your target audience, and ask yourself, "What works have most influenced my audience?"

Let's say you're writing to a young teen audience. You might decide that the huge blockbuster movies of the past decade have been *Harry Potter*; *The Lion, the Witch, and the Wardrobe*; *Pirates of the Caribbean*; *Shrek*; *Spiderman*, and so on. You can then look at television—*Heroes*, *Buffy*, *Spongebob*. You might go on to consider videogames, popular music, and the effect that the twin towers has had on the life of a person growing up today.

In short, as you write, you need to be aware of what your reader has probably been influenced by, and then consider whether or not you want to change what you'd like to write in order to better reach a large potential audience.

Resonance Outside of Tolkien

It may sound as if I've been pretty exhaustive in my dissecting of Tolkien, but I've hardly touched the surface.

Masters at the use of resonance make it a life study.

If you take any major motion picture and study it closely, you will most likely see how it resonates.

For example, if you watch the movie *Avatar*, you can see plot devices that make it feel like *Dances with Wolves* meets *Fern Gully*. Portions of the plot seem to be drawn from a short story by Poul Anderson. Images from the film echo other science fiction movies— from *Alien*, to *Star Trek*, to *2001: A Space Odyssey*, and so on. A couple of characters created for the movie look suspiciously similar to characters from popular videogames. Lines from *Avatar* draw from President George Bush and from the movie the *Terminator*.

If we studied the music, dialog, plotline, ship design, clothing design, and imagery frame-by-frame, we could see how this film ties into dozens of other major franchises.

Was any of it by accident? No. The best writers and directors are painfully conscious about the works that they're struggling to resonate with. They're aware that every piece of literature is part of a greater field of art, and that artists communicate to the world across the generations by joining that conversation.

Recently, I showed some of my students the animated Disney film *Tangled*, and we studied how animators had made it resonate with dozens of other films, many within Disney's own franchises. In some ways, animated films—which one might imagine would be the simplest forms of entertainment—can become more complex and self-conscious than works in just about any medium.

Resonance and You

At this point some readers may feel like I'm telling them all to write like Tolkien, to master the use of resonance down to the level of the ceneme. In actuality, I don't think you need to try to write just like Tolkien—or anyone else.

The truth is that when we try to "create" stories, generally we are simply combining rather common elements. In other words, your story will draw upon the power of resonance whether you mean for it to or not. You'll combine elements that you love from other arts, from other works, and other lives in order to create something extraordinary.

For this reason, I sometimes suggest that authors try to "marry" uncommon elements. Years ago, one of my young students, Stephenie Meyer, asked "How do I become the bestselling young adult writer of all time." So we began discussing what her story would be about—a tale that brought together a sense of wonder and romance. As she talked, she sparked ideas on where she might go with this, speaking about her home in Forks, Washington and vampires in the woods. I recall it vividly because I had lived in such a forest in Oregon about ten years earlier, and I realized that, "Yes, it would be a perfect place for vampires." Her ideas seemed to be vague still, unformed. I warned her that it might be hard to sell such a novel at that time. Major publishers didn't have any lines for contemporary teen fantasy, and even though a romance made sense from a greenlighting aspect, publishers who'd never printed such books might not back it, but I suspected that with the rise of Harry Potter's popularity, the major publishers might be looking for something like Stephenie's books in a few years.

Like many authors, Stephenie's world came together in a vivid dream, and she was able to jump into the project at just the right time. She created a work that resonated with many other things—the works of Anne Rice, the television series *Buffy the Vampire Slayer*, and of course it resonated with Stephenie's own life and the experiences of any teen who goes to a new school.

So dig deep into your own personal experiences, but also learn to tap into cultural phenomenon—into myths, religion, global politics, major motion pictures and books, and even internet memes in order to establish resonance. Draw from the whole of your life, and from the rest of the world.

Where Resonance Goes Wrong

You can't get rid of resonance. Your personal tastes are going to be influenced by the stories that you've loved the most. So don't ever try to be "completely" original. It's a good way to go mad.

I'm reminded of Larry Niven. A critic once talked to him about his bestselling novel *Ringworld,* pointing out that it had strong ties in its plot line to *The Wizard of Oz.* Larry, who is a genius by any standard, was floored. He said, "I suddenly realized that I had read *The Wizard of Oz* hundreds of times as a child. I loved it. Of course, I couldn't help the fact that it helped form my fiction."

Because Niven was drawing upon a popular source for inspiration, it probably helped him to find a large audience.

But let's say that he hadn't. What if, as a child, Larry Niven had fallen in love with a terribly obscure tale. Let's make up one. We'll call it "How Pollywog Lost his Tail." It's the story of a pollywog in a tiny pond. Day by day, the fierce sun beats down upon it, shrinking the pond. As he goes about feeding, he worries that he is going to die, and his tail shrinks. Yet as it shrinks, he finds that he begins to grow new hands and legs. Eventually, the pond dries up, and as the pollywog begins to die, his tail shrinks completely. The pollywog turns into a full-fledged frog, and uses his newfound powers to hop away.

Instead of writing *Ringworld*, let's say that Niven wrote a story about a young lizard man in a city. As city violence escalates, lizard-boy finds that his tail begins shrinking. Eventually, lizard-boy is on the verge of losing his life, when suddenly his "death fangs" grow in, and he gains super powers.

Would the second tale resonate with a larger audience? Not at all. I'm not aware of any place in literature where humans celebrate the loss of body parts as they metamorph into adult creatures. So there hasn't traditionally been an audience for this, and the new novel most likely would never find an audience.

In other words, you can also go wrong by drawing upon obscure sources for your resonance. If you don't develop mainstream tastes at any time of your life, it's not likely that you'll attract a mainstream audience.

This doesn't mean that you can't have a career as an author. It just means that you'll need to try to use your novelty and perhaps your own unique writing skills to create an audience.

A similar thing happens if you don't draw upon common cultural experiences in order to resonate with life. If your life was a novel—if you were raised by lions in Africa—you're not going to be able to draw upon family life, school, and so on in order to create a bond between you and your audience.

Have you ever noticed that very young authors, regardless of talent, can almost never connect to a vast audience? They haven't lived enough, experienced enough, to do so. Given this, they almost always find that they connect with audiences that they do have something in common with—very young audiences.

In Conclusion

We have a vast reservoir of shared experience that helps us as people bond together.

Some of that shared experience can be found in literature, in film, in movies, or in art. Other shared experiences come from our schooling, our workplace, our love of sports— our basic lifestyles.

When you read a popular book or go to a major movie, you're doing it with perhaps millions of other people. You might read a book and find that you enter a magical world, becoming another person for a while. Millions of others do it, too, and the experience changes you all, binds you together. If you're a Star Trek fan, you might travel halfway around the world, meet someone wearing Spock ears in Korea, and instantly feel an affinity for that person. Societies are built around our shared moments.

The truth is that you can't write any tale without drawing upon that vast pool of shared experiences, but the wisest writers, those who become most popular, learn to draw upon art and literature in order to create works that speak to audiences more strongly, more deeply, and appeal to a wider network of readers.

Learn to do draw upon other works consciously, and to do it well. Too often, authors are content to write "little" stories, tales that are so personal that the rest of the world just doesn't relate.

Remember, a great tale isn't just about you. Ultimately, the reader should close your book and feel that a connection has been made, to realize with wonder and delight that "This story is about me."

Ways to Draw Upon Resonance

If you're a novelist, familiarize yourself with the bestselling novels in your genre. Are you trying to write children's books? Then you should read *The Wizard of Oz* and *Alice in Wonderland* in order to get some historical perspective.

In fact, as a writer you need to keep your finger on the pulse of your marketplace, studying all sorts of trends in fiction and fashion.

I once worked with a writer in Hollywood to create a new fantasy franchise. The first thing that he did was ask for a list of other films in the genre that were influential. He then went out and rented movies—*Conan the Barbarian, Willow, Ladyhawke*—and dozens of others, then watched them over the course of several days in order to educate himself about the genre.

Every novelist should do the same, familiarizing himself with popular books, movies, poems, music and other forms of popular art. Depending upon the genre, you may need to research history or videogames.

Beyond other works of art, you need to look at real life. This might mean that you will want to draw from historical records when describing life in Chicago in 1920. You may be able to find old photographs, or read from local writers of the time in order to get a deeper feel for what you're trying to create. You may want to study menus from restaurants in order to get a feel for the cuisine. In order to write about a wizard who used herbs once, I planted a garden with herbs that had historic uses—and then took took the herbs myself, in order to study their effects fist-hand.

In short, as an author, research the work of others. Don't be content to just try to absorb familiar works like a sponge. It's helpful to sit down and research the works of others, to think about their achievements, to study, to garner what you can, and then to use their skills to embellish your own fine creations.

Learn more on how to improve your writing and enhance your stories from David Farland's other writing books:

MILLION DOLLAR OUTLINES

BY DAVID FARLAND

Attend one of David Farland's writing workshops to further hone your craft. View upcoming workshops at www.DavidFarland.net.

6589392R00056

Printed in Great Britain
by Amazon.co.uk, Ltd.,
Marston Gate.